Snakes

Snakes

FROM VIPERS TO BOA CONSTRICTORS

JULIANNA PHOTOPOULOS

amber
BOOKS

Published by Amber Books Ltd
United House
North Road
London
N7 9DP
United Kingdom
www.amberbooks.co.uk
Instagram: amberbooksltd
Facebook: amberbooks
Twitter: @amberbooks
Pinterest: amberbooksltd

ISBN: 978-1-83886-284-8

Project Editor: Michael Spilling
Designer: Keren Harragan
Picture Research: Justin Willsdon

Printed in China

Contents

Introduction

Snakes don't have the best reputation – with lots of us finding these long and limbless, slithering lizards scary. But you may be surprised to learn that snakes actually fear us more than we do them. In fact, snakes will often go out of their way to avoid us. When our paths do cross, they tend to flee, or warn us to stay away, rather than fight. Their fierce stare may seem threatening but that's only because snakes do not have eyelids and cannot blink!

There are close to 4,000 different species of these scaly, cold-blooded animals slithering about on every continent except Antartica. About 600 species are venomous, and only about 200 are able to kill or seriously harm a human.

From the worm-like threadsnakes to enormous pythons, snakes display exceptionally diverse colours, patterns and behaviours. And though all snakes use their forked tongues to smell, some have extra-special senses to help them find their prey. Some snakes then use venom, while others tightly squeeze prey to death – but almost all swallow their food whole. Come, let's explore their fascinating world!

ABOVE:
The rainbow boa (*Epicrates cenchria*) is one of the most spectacular boa species in the world. These brightly coloured snakes are found mostly in humid woodlands and rainforests of South America.

OPPOSITE:
The rough green snake (*Opheodrys aestivus*) is a non-venomous snake found in North America.

Europe

The small European continent – extending from the Arctic to the Mediterranean Sea and bordering Asia with Russia, Ukraine and Turkey – is home to at least 84 snake species. But not every country in Europe has snakes, or lots of them. For example, no snakes can be found in Ireland and Iceland, while Great Britain only has three snakes: the barred grass snake, the smooth snake and the common European adder. And as the name suggests, the latter, which is found from Great Britain to East Asia, is one of the most common snakes in Europe. However, most species on this continent belong to the largest snake family, called Colubridae, or colubrids, which are either harmless or else have venomous fangs at the back of their mouths that pose no danger to us. Only members of the Viperidae or viper family, such as the common European adder, are truly venomous with their long, front-hinged fangs. These snakes also have mesmerizing, zigzag patterns on their backs and distinctive triangular-shaped heads.

Other popular European snakes include the grass snake, noted for playing dead when threatened, and the Caspian whipsnake, which is thought to be the longest snake on this continent.

OPPOSITE:
Aesculapian snake
The non-venomous species
Zamenis longissimus is among the
largest in Europe, reaching up to
2m (6.6ft) in length. Its common
name is derived from Asclepius,
the ancient Greek god of medicine.

ABOVE TOP AND BOTTOM:
Dahl's whip snake
This harmless and fast-moving species, *Platyceps najadum*, rarely grows over 1m (3.3ft) in length. It has distinct black spots, ringed with white, down the side of the neck. *P. najadum* is native to Eurasia, spreading from the Balkans, Turkey and Cyprus to the Middle East, and as far as Turkmenistan and the Caucasus Mountains.

OPPOSITE:
A mass of grass snakes
The mating season, from March to June, sometimes brings grass snakes together in large groups, usually with many males writhing around the larger female. During mating, a male curls its body around a female.

ABOVE TOP AND BOTTOM:
Barred grass snake
Until 2017, grass snakes found in the United Kingdom, Switzerland, France, Italy and western Germany were considered to be the subspecies *Natrix natrix helvetica*. Now, they are a separate species called *Natrix helvetica* or barred grass snake. Like the grass snake, the barred grass snake has a distinctive black and yellow or whitish collar around its neck.

RIGHT:
Grass snake
The Eurasian non-venomous species *Natrix natrix* is found near water, mainly preying on amphibians like frogs. When threatened, grass snakes are known to secrete a foul smell and taste, or play dead.

OPPOSITE (ALL PHOTOGRAPHS):

Caspian whipsnake
This species, *Dolichophis caspius*, spreads across the Balkans and parts of Eastern Europe. Its back is grey-brown, while its front is light yellow or white. At about 1.4–1.6m (4.6–5.2ft) long, the Caspian whipsnake is also known as the large whipsnake.

LEFT:
Defensive posture
Though not venomous, if threatened, the Caspian whipsnake will defend itself by raising its body, hissing loudly and pretending to attack. However, it will bite quickly and without warning if caught or stepped on.

Mating ball
These numerous entwined snakes, known as the dice snake or *Natrix tessellata*, gather together to mate in the springtime. In the summer, females lay clutches of 10–30 eggs.

Keeping warm
A barred grass snake basks on autumnal leaves in the British woods. After lunch, snakes usually bask to raise their body temperature, until digestion is complete. However, when temperatures start to drop, barred grass snakes search for refuge to keep their bodies warm through the winter.

OPPOSITE:

Montpellier snake
This mildly venomous juvenile snake, *Malpolon monspessulanus*, can reach up to 2m (7ft) long. Younger snakes have a conspicuous blotched or spotted pattern, including a darker pattern on the head than adults. Montpellier snakes are common throughout Spain, Portugal, the southern coast of France and northwest Africa.

LEFT TOP AND BOTTOM:

Ladder snake
Zamenis scalaris is a non-venomous species found in southwestern Europe. Only young snakes have the distinctive black ladder pattern on their backs. This pattern gradually fades and adults are left with two dark stripes running down neck-to-tail.

ABOVE TOP:
Western whip snake
The species *Hierophis viridiflavus* is also known as the green whip snake due to its greenish-yellow colour and irregular dark green or black bands. However, this subspecies of the western whip snake, *Hierophis viridiflavus carbonarius*, is entirely black. It is found only in southern Italy, Croatia, the Greek island of Gyaros, and Malta.

ABOVE BOTTOM:
European worm snake
This blind snake, *Xerotyphlops vermicularis*, somewhat resembles an earthworm. Despite its common name, the European worm snake – or European blind snake – lives in Europe and Asia, spreading from Southeastern Europe to Afghanistan.

RIGHT:
Armenian viper
Named after the German naturalist Gustav Radde, this subspecies, *Montivipera raddei raddei*, is common in the mountainous areas of Armenia, Azerbaijan, eastern Turkey, northwest Iran, and Turkmenistan. Like all members of the Viperidae family, commonly known as vipers, they are venomous.

Dice snake
Natrix tessellata, or the dice snake, is a harmless water snake that lives across most of Europe and Asia. Like its cousin, *Natrix natrix*, it secretes a bad smell and can play dead as a defence. Dice snakes are excellent swimmers and feed only on fish and amphibians.

ABOVE:
European cat snake
This snake, *Telescopus fallax*, is found across the Mediterranean and the Caucasus Mountains. Though venomous, it has its fangs at the back of the upper jaw, making it difficult to inject venom into humans. Its venom, however, does work on its prey, such as lizards. It gets its name from its cat-like eyes.

RIGHT:
Ready to attack
The mildly venomous eastern Montpellier snake, or *Malpolon insignitus*, will defend itself if needed. When alarmed, it raises its head, flattens its neck and hisses.

OPPOSITE:
Eastern Montpellier snake
Not only can these snakes move fast, swim and climb, but they also have good eyesight. Their skin is waterproof and heatproof thanks to the liquid secreted by the two large glands located under their skin between the eyes and nostrils.

Ottoman viper
Montivipera xanthina is known by many names: rock viper, coastal viper, Turkish viper, mountain viper and Ottoman viper. This aggressive and very venomous snake has a distinct dark brown-black zigzag pattern on its back. *M. xanthina* lives in rocky and well-vegetated habitats across northeastern Greece, Turkey, and some Aegean islands.

ALL PHOTOGRAPHS:
Common European adder
This widespread venomous species, *Vipera berus*, lives across most of Europe and reaches East Asia. It can be recognized by the zigzag pattern along the back of its body and tail, the distinctive 'V' or 'X' on its head, and a dark streak from the eye to its neck. Males are grey with black markings, whilst females are usually brown with dark brown markings.

Four-lined snake

As its name suggests, the four-lined snake, or *Elaphe quatuorlineata*, has four dark stripes running down its yellowish-brown body. However, only the adults live up to this name, with juveniles having a different pattern. The non-venomous four-lined snake is one of the largest European snakes, spreading across Italy and most of Southeastern Europe.

LEFT:

Shedding

A harmless southern smooth
snake, or *Coronella girondica*,
sheds its skin in a process called
ecdysis. As a snake's body
continues to grow, its old skin layer
is replaced with a new one. By
rubbing against rough surfaces like
rocks, the snake tears the old layer
off. Snakes can shed their skin
4–12 times per year.

ABOVE:

Viperine water snake

This non-venomous snake, *Natrix
maura*, can be found in rivers and
lakes of southwestern Europe and
northwestern Africa. Resembling
its close relative, the grass snake,
the viperine water snake spends
most of its time in the water
preying on fish and frogs.

OPPOSITE TOP:
Steppe rat snake
Named after Dione, the mother of the Greek goddess Aphrodite, *Elaphe dione* lives in eastern Europe and Asia. It is commonly known as the steppe rat snake, and has a distinctive W-shaped pattern on its head.

OPPOSITE BOTTOM:
Red whip snake
Often confused with Dahl's whip snake, this harmless colubrid species, *Platyceps collaris*, has a smaller, flatter head. *P. collaris* can reach up to 70cm (2.3ft) long in Europe, but can grow even longer (1m or 3.3ft) in Asia.

LEFT AND BELOW:
Nose-horned viper
The venomous species *Vipera ammodytes*, from southern Europe, is the most dangerous of the European vipers. It prefers rocky habitats, despite its specific name *ammodytes* meaning 'sand-diver' in Greek. Instead, its name nose-horned viper is much more apt, it having a conspicuous horn on its snout that can grow to about 5mm (0.2in).

Blotched snake
This captivating species, *Elaphe sauromates*, can grow to 2.6m (8.5ft), making it one of the largest snakes in the European continent. Young snakes have conspicuous large black-brown blotches on their backs that get fainter over time.

LEFT:
Javelin sand boa
The species *Eryx jaculus* is found in Eastern Europe, the Caucasus, the Middle East and northern Africa. Unlike most snakes, it does not lay eggs but gives birth to live young that can grow to 80cm (31.5in) long.

ABOVE TOP:
Milos viper
This endangered venomous viper, *Macrovipera schweizeri*, lives on four small Greek islands of the Cyclades: Milos, Sifnos, Kimolos and Polyaigos. It is often found in ravines and rocky areas with bushes, where it ambushes migratory birds.

ABOVE BOTTOM:
Leopard snake
As its name suggests, the non-venomous leopard snake (*Zamenis situla*) has black-bordered reddish or brown blotches, which makes it resemble a leopard. However, it can sometimes also have stripes instead of blotches.

Africa

About 500 snake species live in Africa, the hottest and second largest continent on our planet. Africa is home to the world's largest desert, the Sahara, and to some of the most dangerous, beautiful and fascinating snakes – from small, harmless species like Peter's threadsnake to the not-so-harmless gigantic Central African rock python and the extremely venomous black mamba.

African snakes can be found in many habitats, from tropical to desert and water. To survive in this continent, snakes have evolved a number of traits: Malagasy leaf-nosed snakes' camouflage is spot on,

Saharan horned vipers slither sideways across the sand, black mambas and the cryptic puff adders and boomslangs have very potent venom, and non-venomous species such as the African rock pythons have a strong grip. Some cobras can also spit to blind predators or attackers, while others, like the Egyptian cobra, can only warn them off with their hissing, large hoods and defensive displays.

Though snakes will usually try to escape when confronted, some will bite when threatened or stepped on – and people most at risk live in poor, rural regions of Africa, where it is really hard for them to get treatment.

OPPOSITE:
Ball python
This striking species, *Python regius*, is native to West and Central Africa. Commonly known as the ball python or royal python, it is the smallest African python, reaching up to 1.82m (6ft) in length. When frightened, the ball python curls into a ball.

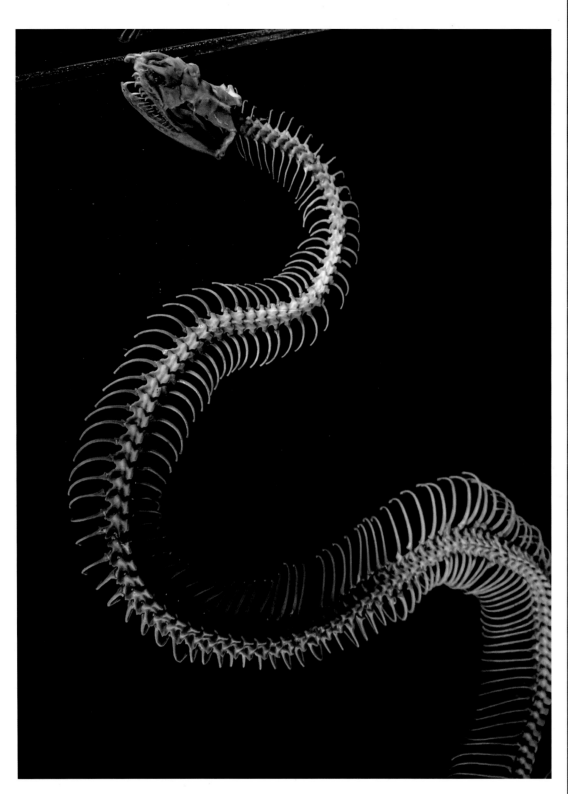

ABOVE:

Lithe skeleton

This skeleton belongs to Africa's longest venomous snake, the black mamba. Black mambas are about 2–3m (6.6–9.8ft) long and spread their cobra-like neck into a hood when alarmed. Their lithe bodies make them very fast and ready to inject venom with their 6.5mm (0.26in)-long fangs, situated in the front of the mouth.

RIGHT:

Black mamba

The lethally venomous species *Dendroaspis polylepis*, or black mamba, lives in the savannahs and rocky hills of southern and eastern Africa. Black mambas are highly aggressive and get their name from the black interior of their mouths, which they display when they are threatened.

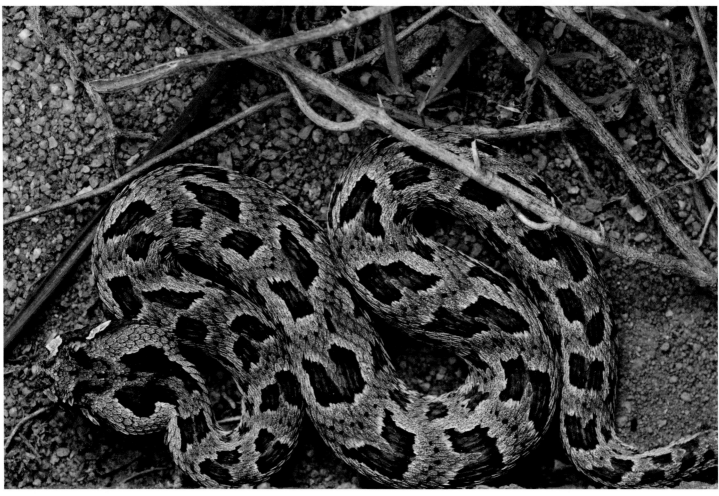

Many-horned adder
As its common name suggests, the many-horned adder, or *Bitis cornuta*, has two to five distinctive horn-like scales above both eyes. Its back is filled with large, dark brown blotches, which resemble squares or parallelograms, with white borders.

LEFT:
Cape cobra
Also known as the yellow cobra, this venomous species, *Naja nivea*, actually varies in its colour: from yellow and gold to brown or even black. It lives in a wide range of habitats across southern Africa.

Eastern green mamba
This elusive species (*Dendroaspis angusticeps*) gets its name from the bright green scales on its back. The green colour helps the snake blend in with its tree-dwelling environment in the coastal regions of southern East Africa. Young snakes, however, are blue-green and become bright green when they reach about 75cm (2.5ft) in length.

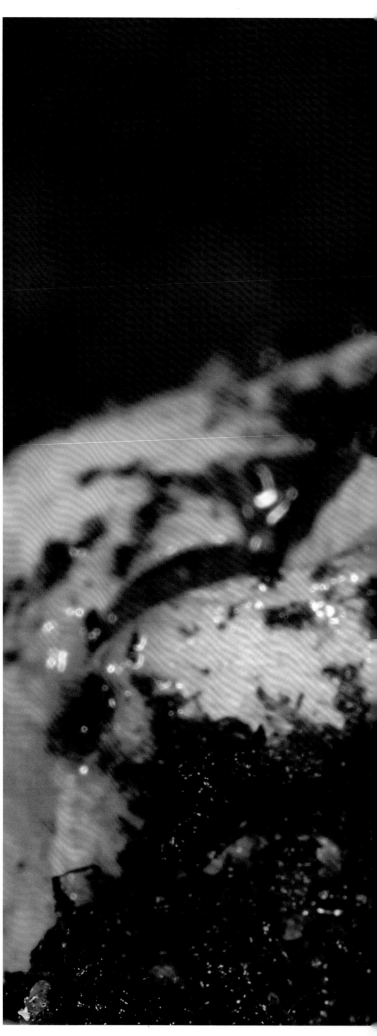

ABOVE TOP AND BOTTOM:

Boomslang

Dispholidus typus is an extremely venomous species from Sub-Saharan Africa. Its name, boomslang, means 'tree snake' in Afrikaans and Dutch. In fact, this snake lives mainly in forested areas and spends most of its time in trees.

RIGHT:

Hatchling

These big, emerald green eyes belong to the deadly boomslang. At about 20cm (7.9in) long, male hatchlings are grey with blue speckles, whilst the females are brown.

Saharan horned viper

Also known as the desert horned viper, this venomous snake gets its name from the horn over each eye. However, sometimes some individuals don't have horns. Saharan horned vipers, or *Cerastes cerastes*, live in the deserts of North Africa and parts of Arabia and the Levant in Western Asia.

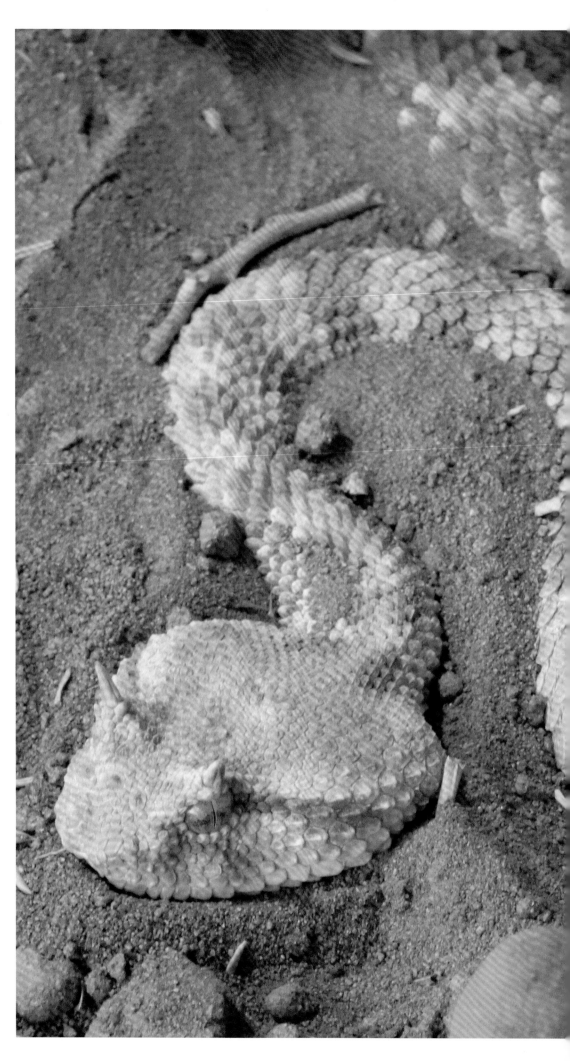

RIGHT:
Kenyan sand boa
Native to northern and eastern Africa, the sand boa (*Eryx colubrinus*) spends most of its time under the sand or soft soil. It has a yellow or orange back with dark brown blotches and a whitish-cream belly.

BELOW:
Green bush viper
As the name suggests, this venomous viper (*Atheris squamigera*) from western and Central Africa is usually some shade of green – the perfect camouflage in the forest.

OPPOSITE:
Hairy bush viper
Named for its bristly hair-like look, the hairy bush viper (*Atheris hispida*) lives in the rainforests and bushes of Central Africa.

Central African egg-eating snake
This tree-dwelling species, *Dasypeltis fasciata*, only eats whole eggs – often several times bigger than its body! To do this, these snakes have no teeth, an extendable neck, and a flattened windpipe that can push around the egg whilst still allowing the snake to breathe.

LEFT:
Squeeze
All pythons are non-venomous constrictors. This means that once they grip prey with their mouths, they wrap their coils around them and squeeze tighter every time the prey breathes out. Here, an African rock python has caught an unwary dove in an acacia tree.

ABOVE TOP:
Central African rock python
The python species *Python sebae* can reach about 6m (20ft) or more, making it Africa's largest snake. Also one of the largest in the world, the Central African rock python resembles its smaller close relative, the Southern African rock python.

ABOVE BOTTOM:
Single gulp
An African rock python devours a gazelle. These snakes kill their prey by constriction and often eat animals up to the size of an antelope – at times, even crocodiles. They could spend weeks digesting such large animals, which are swallowed whole.

OPPOSITE:
Egyptian cobra
This large species, *Naja haje*, is one of the most venomous snakes in North Africa. With an average length of 1.4m (4.6ft), the Egyptian cobra has a stout body and a long tail. It is also known as Ouraeus – an upright snake symbol in Egyptian mythology that represented divine authority.

LEFT TOP, MIDDLE AND BOTTOM:
Egg eater
The common egg-eating snake, or *Dasypeltis scabra*, feeds exclusively on eggs. To swallow an egg, the snake holds it against its body, widens its jaws and slowly stretches the skin of its head around the egg. At the back of the throat, there are sharp protrusions that puncture the shell. The egg contents end up in the snake's belly, while the shell is expelled from its mouth.

OPPOSITE TOP AND ABOVE:
Eyelash bush viper
The Tanzanian viper *Atheris ceratophora* is known for its set of three to five horn-like scales above each eye, resembling eyelashes. Its colour can vary from a yellowish-green or olive to a grey or black, sometimes covered with markings.

LEFT:
Malagasy leaf-nosed snake
This bizarre-looking species gets its name from the flattened, leaf-like protrusion on its snout. However, only the greyish females live up to the name, while males have a long pointed snout. Malagasy leaf-nosed snakes, or *Langaha madagascariensis*, live in the forests of Madagascar.

Puff adder

Don't let its gaze fool you. Found in savannahs and grasslands, this aggressive species (*Bitis arietans*) is responsible for causing the most snakebite deaths in Africa. The specific name *arietans* is derived from the Latin for 'striking violently'. When threatened, it hisses and puffs continuously and sits in an S-shaped position, ready to strike.

RIGHT TOP:

Western green mamba

This long, agile and extremely venomous green snake, *Dendroaspis viridis*, lives in western Africa. It spends most of its time in trees, though it will occasionally come down to hunt on the ground. When threatened, western green mambas flatten their neck into a slight hood.

RIGHT MIDDLE:

Striped house snake

At about 15cm (5.9in) long, this hatchling belongs to the species *Boaedon lineatus* and is known as the striped house snake. Widespread across Africa, from Tanzania through Central Africa to Uganda, females will reach about 1m (3.3ft) in length, whilst males rarely exceed 60cm (1.97ft).

RIGHT BOTTOM:

Yellow-bellied sea snake

As the name suggests, this venomous sea snake has a distinctive yellow belly and a brown back. The yellow-bellied sea snake, or *Hydrophis platurus*, lives in tropical seas around the world except for the Atlantic Ocean. It mates in warm waters and gives birth to live young.

OPPOSITE:

Southern African rock python

Known to grow to more than 5m (16ft), the species *Python natalensis* is one of the largest in the world. It is native to Southern Africa, as its common name suggests, and lives in savannahs and woodlands.

ABOVE TOP:
Vine snakes
Members of the *Thelotornis* genus are known as twig or vine snakes. These are slender, tree-dwelling snakes with a pointed snout and keyhole-shaped pupils. Their cryptic colours and ability to freeze or sway gently make them look like a twig or vine on a tree.

ABOVE BOTTOM:
Peter's threadsnake
This harmless worm-like species, *Leptotyphlops scutifrons*, lives mostly underground in countries of Southern Africa. Peter's threadsnakes feed on invertebrates, especially termites and their eggs, and grow to about 20cm (7.9in).

OPPOSITE:
Madagascar tree boa
The beautiful non-venomous species *Sanzinia madagascariensis* is usually found in trees or bushes near water, on the island of Madagascar. Madagascar, or Malagasy, tree boas are born red, but their colour changes to green as they mature.

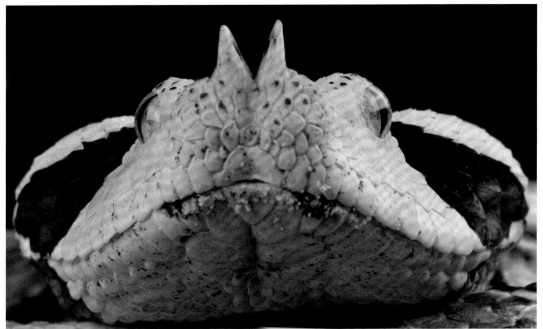

OPPOSITE:
Rhinoceros viper
The beautiful, venomous species *Bitis nasicornis* is a close relative of the Gabino viper. Both have prominent horns, but the rhinoceros viper – also known as the butterfly viper – has a brighter colour pattern and narrower head. It lives in the forests of West and Central Africa.

LEFT TOP AND BOTTOM:
Gabino viper
This West African venomous viper, also known as the West African Gaboon viper and *Bitis rhinoceros*, has two distinctive horns on its snout and one black triangle under each eye.

ABOVE TOP AND BOTTOM:
Spotted bush snake
This harmless green snake with black speckles can be found in the trees of African bushes and forests, preying on lizards or treefrogs. In addition to being an exceptional climber, the spotted bush snake, or *Philothamnus semivariegatus*, is also a good swimmer and is extremely alert.

RIGHT:
Snakeskin
A young spotted bush snake sits with its shedded skin, covered in detailed patterns, in South Africa. Snakes rub against rough surfaces to shed their old skin, which is much longer than the snake itself. This is because the skin covers the entire scale from top to bottom.

Asia

Stretching from the eastern Mediterranean Sea to the western Pacific Ocean, Asia is the largest continent. Some of its countries are among the most populated in the world. One-third of snake species also live on this continent, including the world's longest snake, the reticulated python, and the longest venomous snake, the king cobra.

Many vibrantly coloured snakes slither about in Asia, too. These unique colours and patterns are often used to hide from predators, lure prey in, or even scare off any threats. For instance, Asian vine snakes' vivid green scales help them blend within trees, while the gold-ringed cat snake, resembling a bumblebee, scares predators away. But, in nature, eye-catching colours also warn others to stay away – usually meaning these snakes are extremely venomous, like the captivating blue Malayan coral snakes or Indonesian pit vipers.

Beautifully patterned are also the saw-scaled vipers, believed to be responsible for more human deaths than all other snake species combined. However, their venom is used to make several drugs, such as blood thinners. Asia is also home to the intriguing, mildly venomous flying or gliding snakes – dangerous only to their small prey, such as mice, birds and bats.

OPPOSITE:
Banded krait
The venomous species *Bungarus fasciatus*, with alternate black and yellow bands, black eyes and yellow lips and throat, lives in India, Southeast Asia and southern China. Reaching up to 2.7m (8.9ft) in length, it is the longest species of krait.

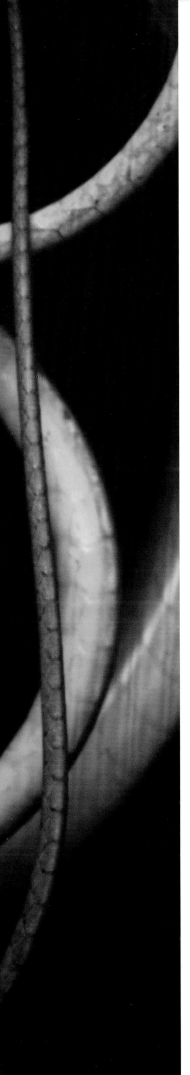

LEFT AND ABOVE TOP:
Asian vine snakes
The staggering members of the *Ahaetulla* genus, commonly known as Asian vine snakes, are noted for their long, slender bodies and keyhole-shaped pupils. They can be found in rainforest trees, from Sri Lanka and India to China and much of Southeast Asia.

ABOVE BOTTOM:
Arabian sand boa
Also known as Jayakar's sand boa or *Eryx jayakari*, this small, harmless desert snake spends its day buried deep under the sands of the Arabian Peninsula and Iran. At dusk, it moves beneath the sand's surface, with only its eyes protruding, ready to pounce on its prey.

OVERLEAF:
Blood python
This striking non-venomous species, *Python brongersmai*, can be found in marshes and tropical swamps in the forests of Southeast Asia. Named after the blood-red markings on its skin, the blood python, or red blood python, is up and about at dusk or dawn.

Deadly fangs

This skeleton belongs to the
longest venomous snake in the
world, the king cobra, which can
reach 5.5m (18ft) in length. It has
two short, fixed fangs in the front
of the mouth that can deliver
enough venom to kill an elephant,
with a single bite.

RIGHT MIDDLE:
King cobra

The threatened, venomous species
Ophiophagus hannah lives
mainly in the forests of South and
Southeast Asia. Its colour varies
across regions and habitats, from
black with white stripes to entirely
brownish-grey.

RIGHT BOTTOM:
Threat display

When disturbed, a king cobra
raises its body, flares out its
hood, shows its fangs and
hisses – a sound almost like that
of a growling dog. Despite its
aggressive reputation, these snakes
are shy and will avoid us whenever
possible. However, king cobras
will attack when cornered.

FAR RIGHT:
Sri Lankan pit viper

As its common name suggests,
this stunning venomous snake is
endemic to Sri Lanka. Its colour
can vary, but usually the species
Craspedocephalus trigonocephalus
is green with a black variegated
pattern, and a black line behind
its eyes.

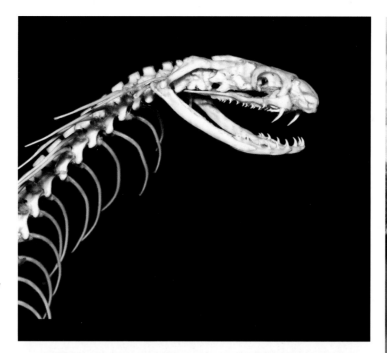

Burmese python
Among the largest species of snakes, *Python bivittatus* can reach 7m (23ft) or more in length and weigh 91kg (200lb). Burmese pythons are native to Southeast Asia and get their name from the country of Burma, now known as Myanmar. Laying clutches of up to 100 eggs, this beautifully patterned female keeps her eggs warm for two to three months, until they hatch.

Green pit viper species

Members of the *Trimeresurus* genus are known as green pit vipers. Though most are typically green, some species do not live up to this name, having yellow, black, orange, red or gold markings.

Striped coral snake

The venomous species *Calliophis nigrescens* spends most of its life underground in the Western Ghats of India. Commonly known as the black coral snake or striped coral snake, it comes in diverse colours and patterns. However, the head and the back of the neck are always black with a diagonal yellow band – sometimes broken up into spots.

Banded Malaysian coral snake

This extremely venomous coral snake, *Calliophis intestinalis*, can be found in the forests of Southeast Asia, hunting in leaf litter at night. Its colour varies from light brown to black but has a distinctive red-orange dorsal stripe, a red tail, and its belly has a black and white pattern that it shows off when it is threatened.

ALL PHOTOGRAPHS:

Common bronzeback
The species *Dendrelaphis tristis*
is a harmless, long and slender
tree-dwelling snake. Also known as
Daudin's bronzeback or common
bronzeback, its back is indeed
a bronze colour, helping it hide
among the trees. Recent research
has found that members of the
Dendrelaphis genus can launch
themselves, or jump, from one tree
to another.

OVERLEAF:

Blue Malayan coral snake
The beautiful tropical coral snake
species, *Calliophis bivirgatus*, is
native to Southeast Asia. It is dark
blue to black – generally with a
broad blue stripe on its sides – and
has a red head, tail and belly. The
venomous blue Malayan coral
snake spends most of its time
amongst the leaf litter of forests
and feeds mainly on other snakes.

Cat-eyed water snake
Found in coastal areas, especially mangroves, between western India to the eastern Philippines, the cat-eyed water snake, or *Gerarda prevostiana*, feeds almost exclusively on crabs. Instead of swallowing them whole, it tears the crab into bite-sized pieces by pulling it through its coils.

Boulenger's bronzeback
This snake, *Dendrelaphis bifrenalis*, lives on the trees, shrubs and bushes of Sri Lanka and the Eastern Ghats of South India. Named after the zoologist George Albert Boulenger, the Boulenger's bronzeback has rougher central-ridged, or keeled, scales on its belly, which help it to climb trees.

LEFT AND BELOW:
Blunt-headed slug-eating snake
This small snake feeds on snails by cutting their shell with its lower jawbones, or mandibles. When threatened, *Aplopeltura boa* coils itself up, showing its belly and playing dead. It lives in Thailand, Malaysia, Indonesia, Brunei and the Philippines.

LEFT:

Beware!

A mangrove snake, or *Boiga dendrophila*, found in Southeast Asia opens its mouth wide as a threat display. Mangrove snakes are nocturnal and have vertical-slit pupils like a cat, giving it the nickname yellow-ringed cat snake. All members of the *Boiga* genus have long bodies with large heads and cat-like eyes.

OVERLEAF ALL PHOTOGRAPHS:

Indian cobra

Also known as the spectacled cobra and *Naja naja*, this venomous snake displays a spectacular hood when threatened. Many Indian cobras have two connected eye-like markings on the back of their hoods, resembling eyeglasses or spectacles.

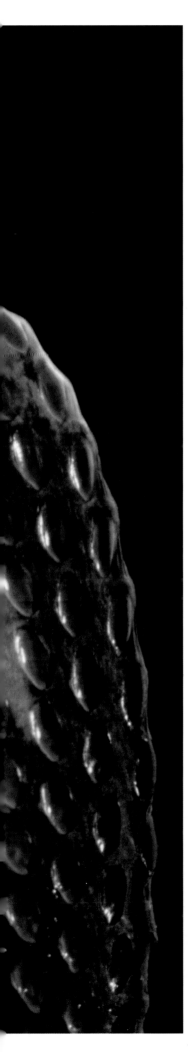
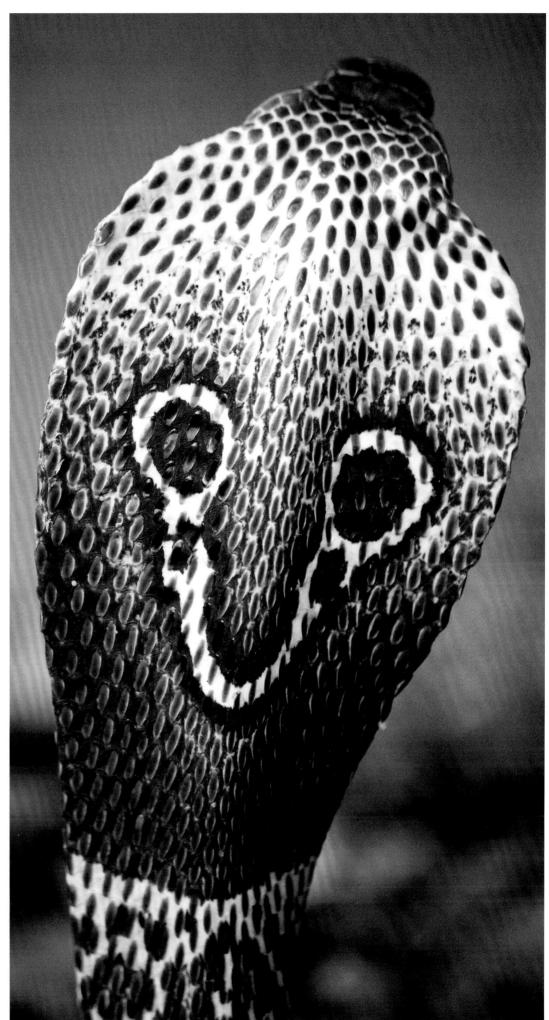

Hagen's pit viper

The venomous species *Trimeresurus hageni*, from Southeast Asia, is named after the German naturalist Bernhard Hagen. It lives on trees thanks to its long prehensile tail, which it uses to grasp tree branches.

Caspian cobra

Also known as the Central Asian cobra, the venomous species *Naja oxiana* is native to Central Asia. For many years, it was erroneously considered a subspecies of the Indian cobra. The Caspian cobra is believed to be the most venomous species of cobra in the world.

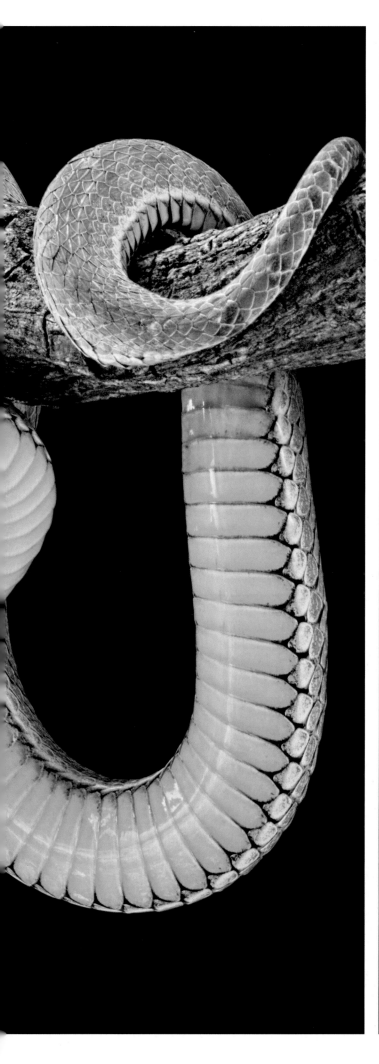

OPPOSITE:
Timor python
This non-venomous constrictor, *Malayopython timoriensis*, kills its prey by pulling it into its ever-tightening coils – like all pythons. It is found in forests and grasslands of the southeastern islands of Indonesia, specifically the Lesser Sunda Islands.

ABOVE TOP:
Painted saw-scaled viper
This well-camouflaged species, *Echis coloratus*, can be found in rocky deserts (not sandy ones) across the Middle East and Egypt, and is extremely venomous.

ABOVE BOTTOM LEFT AND RIGHT:
Saw-scaled vipers
Members of the *Echis* genus are known as saw-scaled vipers. This is because some of the scales on their body stick out and are saw-like. These extremely venomous vipers have a distinctive threat display, in which they form parallel coils and rub their scales together to make a sizzling sound.

Skeleton

Without any legs or arms, snakes have simple skeletons. Their skull is attached to a long and flexible spine, which allows them to bend and curl. With hundreds of floating ribs along their bodies, they can expand to the size of their prey – sometimes much bigger than their heads! This skeleton belongs to the Indian python.

Indian python

The large yet shy species *Python molurus* lives near water in India and several surrounding countries. It moves slowly, usually in a straight line, and rarely attacks – even when attacked. Often confused with the Burmese python, the Indian python is usually lighter in colour.

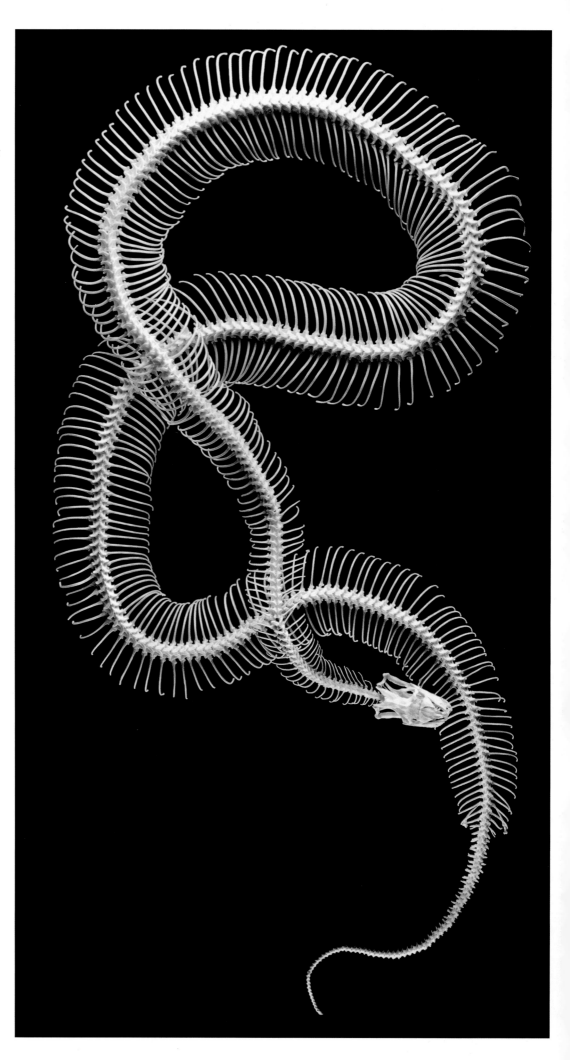

ABOVE BOTTOM:
Sand boa
Native to Iran, Pakistan and India, the species *Eryx johnii* can grow to more than 1.22m (4ft), making it the longest sand boa. Its colour varies from a yellow-tan to a reddish brown.

ABOVE TOP AND RIGHT:
Indian rat snake
The species *Ptyas mucosa* from South and Southeast Asia can make a growling sound and expand its neck when threatened – just like the king cobra or Indian cobra. However, the Indian rat snake, or oriental rat snake, is harmless. Even when two males are fighting to pursue a female, it looks like they are dancing as they intertwine their long, slender bodies.

LEFT:
Golden tree snake
This stunning, fast-moving species, *Chrysopelea ornata*, lives in trees of South and Southeast Asia. Like other members of the *Chrysopelea* genus, the golden tree snake is an excellent climber and can launch itself into the air and glide, or parachute, from tree to tree.

ABOVE TOP:
Squeeze play
Golden tree snakes are mildly venomous and it takes some time to kill fast-moving prey, such as lizards and rodents. So, after sinking their fangs into their prey and injecting a dose of venom, they wrap themselves around them and squeeze to prevent them from escaping. Here, a golden tree snake wraps its muscular coils around a butterfly lizard.

ABOVE BOTTOM:
Gulping down
A golden tree snake devours a large butterfly lizard. Once the prey has been killed, snakes can swallow their meal whole. This is because they can open their jaws much wider than their bodies or heads, thanks to the loosely hinged jaws, which can move independently.

OPPOSITE:

Beautiful pit viper
The extremely venomous species *Trimeresurus venustus* can be found only in a few areas of southern Thailand. Commonly known as the beautiful pit viper or brown-spotted pit viper, this snake is as deadly as it is stunning.

ABOVE AND LEFT:

Fea's vipers
Members of the *Azemiops* genus are known as Fea's vipers, or Burmese vipers. These rare, pitless vipers comprise two species: *A. feae*, or black-headed Fea's viper, and *A. kharini* or white-headed Fea's viper.

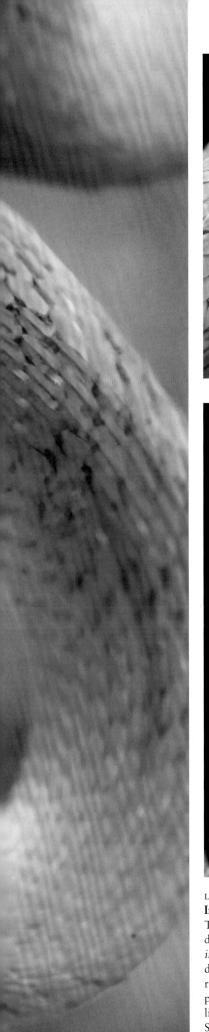

LEFT:
Indonesian pit viper
This stunningly blue, island-dwelling species, *Trimeresurus insularis*, is both aggressive and deadly. The blue variant is quite rare as, in fact, most Indonesian pit vipers are green. These snakes live in eastern Java and the Lesser Sunda Islands of Indonesia and East Timor.

ABOVE TOP:
Yellow morph
Besides blue and green, the venomous Indonesian pit viper – also known as the Sunda white-lipped pit viper – can also be found in yellow. It lives in trees and eats birds, frogs and small mammals.

ABOVE BOTTOM:
Wagler's pit viper
Native to forests of Southeast Asia, the venomous species *Tropidolaemus Wagleri* is named after the German herpetologist Johann Georg Wagler. Males are green, while this black snake with yellow stripes is a female.

RIGHT TOP:

Malayan bridle snake

The relatively small species *Lycodon subannulatus* has a slender body, resembling a horse's leather strap, or bridle. It is an excellent climber and can easily grip a tree trunk. The Malayan bridle snake can be found in forests of Southeast Asia.

RIGHT MIDDLE:

Malayan krait

This species of Southeast Asia, *Bungarus candidus*, is a very venomous snake. Commonly known as the Malayan krait or blue krait, it has an alternate pattern of dark brown, black or bluish-black and yellowish-white bands on its back.

RIGHT BOTTOM:

Many-banded krait

Also known as the Chinese krait and *Bungarus multicinctus*, the many-banded krait can be found in China and Southeast Asia. It has many alternate white and black or bluish-black bands across its body.

OPPOSITE:

Monocled cobra

The venomous species *Naja kaouthia* lives in South and Southeast Asia. The monocled cobra, also known as the Indian spitting cobra and monocellate cobra, has an O-shaped pattern on the back of its hood, resembling a single eye or monocellate.

OVERLEAF:

Sexual dimorphism

It is easy to distinguish between male and female Wagler's pit vipers: the green males have a relatively slender body with a large triangular head, while females are black with yellow stripes and are slightly longer than males. Here, a close-up of a male Wagler's pit viper shows its green scales and pits, or openings, between the eyes and nostril.

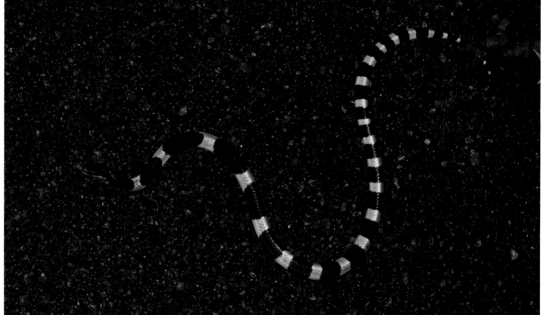

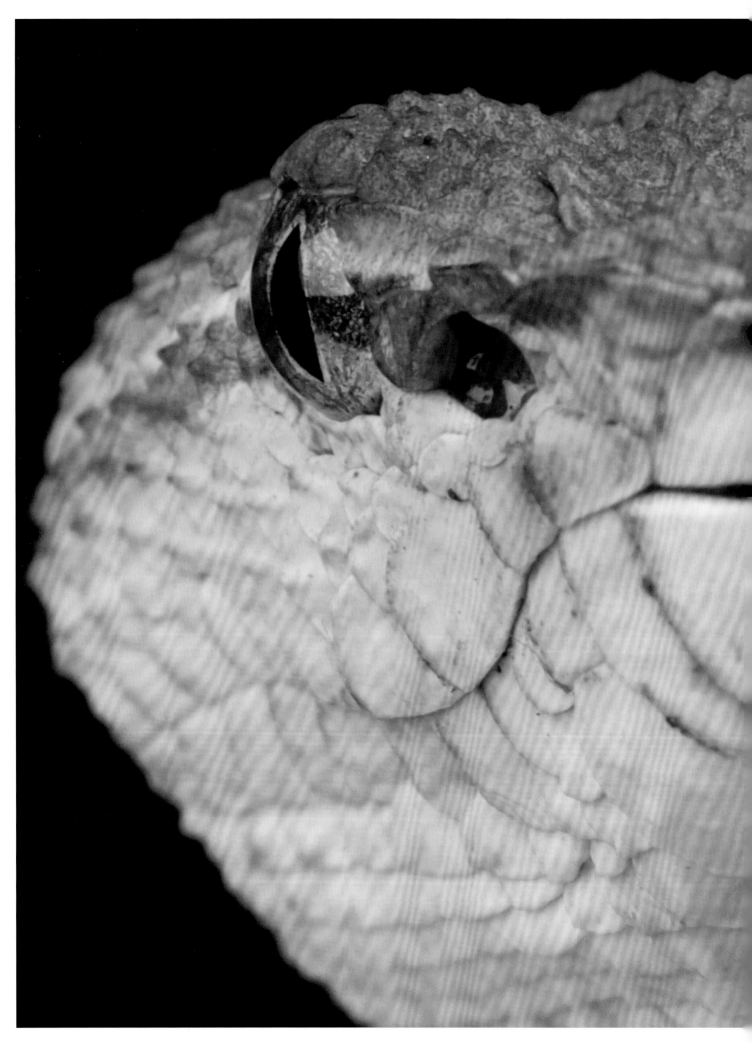

Paradise tree snake

Also known as the paradise flying snake, this exquisite, tree-dwelling species, *Chrysopelea paradisi*, can glide 10m (33ft) or more from a treetop. It does this by flattening its body, then swinging and making snake-like movements in mid-air whilst keeping its head quite stable.

Black-headed cat snake

The species *Boiga nigriceps* of Southeast Asian gets its name from its dark, almost black, head. However, only the adults live up to this name. Here, a red juvenile black-headed cat snake feeds on a lizard.

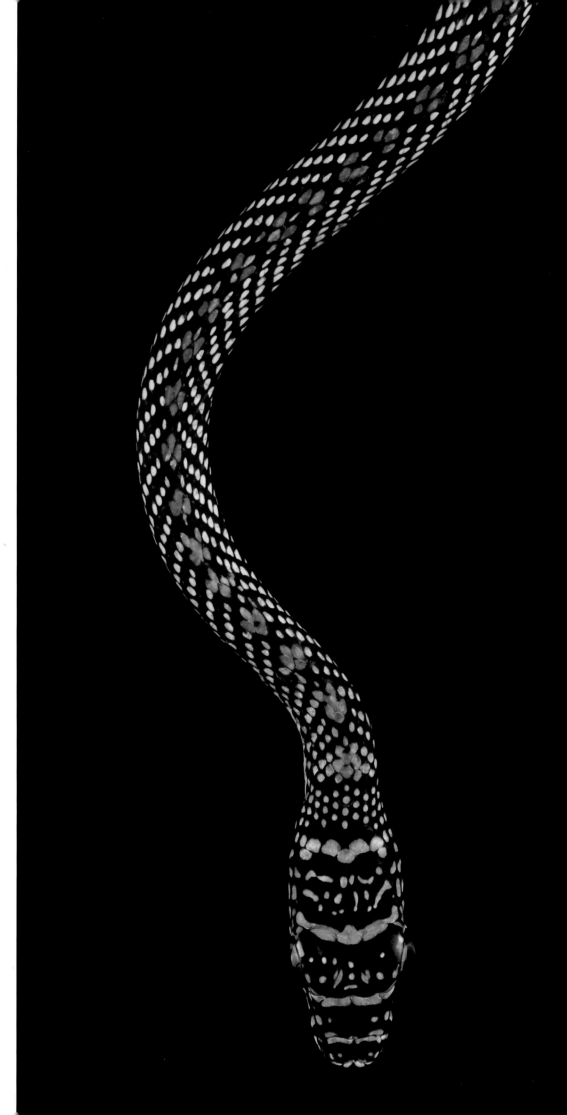

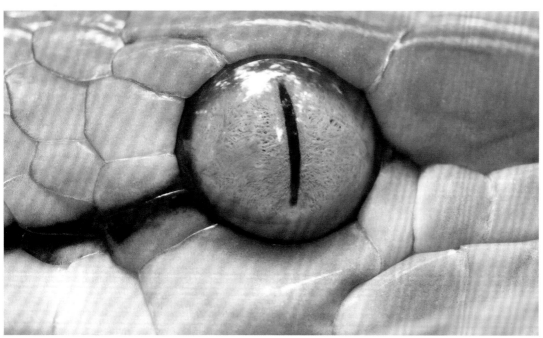

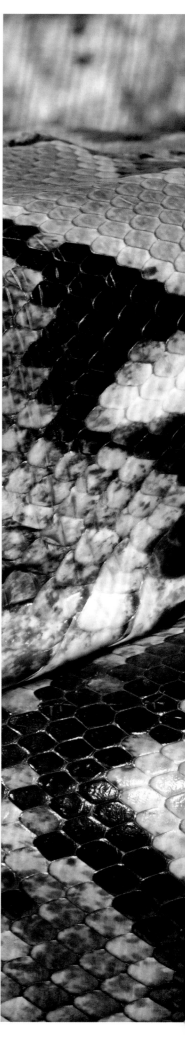

ABOVE TOP:
New life
At least 61cm (2ft) long, this reticulated python emerges from its egg. The watery fluid within the egg protects the snake from injury and from drying out while hatching. To break the eggshell, it uses the sharp egg tooth on its upper lip.

ABOVE BOTTOM:
Vision
This dazzling orange eye with a vertical-slit pupil belongs to the reticulated python. Snakes that are active at night usually have such cat-like, or elliptical, pupils, while round pupils belong to daytime snakes. But pythons cannot see very well so have many openings lining their lips, called pit organs, which help them to 'see' the heat of their warm-blooded prey.

RIGHT:
Reticulated python
The captivating net-like, or reticulated, patterned skin gives this python its name. The reticulated python, or *Malayopython reticulatus*, lives in South and Southeast Asia. It is the longest snake in the world, reaching over 6m (20ft) in length.

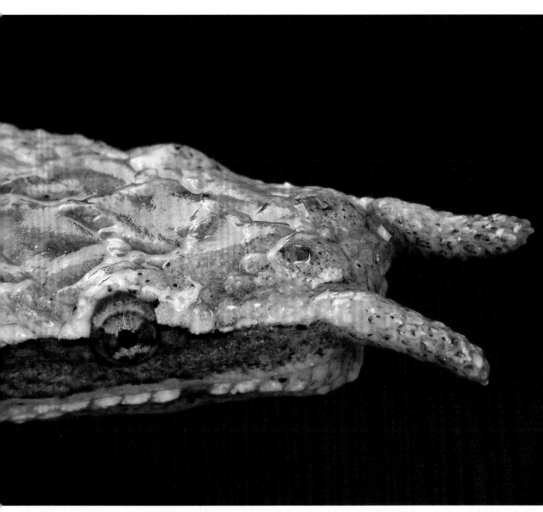

LEFT:
Tentacled snake
Native to Southeast Asia, the alien-looking species *Erpeton tentaculatum* lives underwater and eats fish. It is named after its two short, scaly tentacles protruding from its snout, which help it to detect prey in muddy water.

OPPOSITE BOTTOM:
Smooth slug snake
As the name suggests, this southeastern Asian snake feeds solely on slugs and snails. More teeth on its lower jaw means the smooth slug snake, or *Asthenodipsas laevis*, can extract snails from their shell. *A. laevis* is brown and somewhat flattened laterally along its body.

BELOW:
Rhinoceros rat snake
This tree-dwelling snake, from northern Vietnam to southern China, is named for its distinctive long, rhinoceros-like snout. The rhinoceros rat snake (*Gonyosoma boulengeri*) is also known as the rhinoceros snake and Vietnamese longnose snake.

Australia

Not to be confused with the country, Australia is the smallest and least populated continent after Antartica. But the continent – which consists of many large and small islands, including Australia, New Guinea, Fiji and other Pacific islands – has more than 170 species of snakes that live on land and in the ocean.

In fact, some of the world's most venomous snakes can be found here, most of which are members of the Elapidae family – commonly known as elapids – that have permanently erect venomous fangs. Here, elapids range from small species that live in hiding, the thickset viper-like ambush predators called death adders, to large and extremely venomous species, such as taipans, brown snakes and tiger snakes. Interestingly, Australia has no vipers and only a few colubrids, which can be venomous, or not at all.

This continent is also home to inconspicuous worm-like blind snakes and magnificent non-venomous pythons that constrict prey in their muscular coils. While the secretive and shy inland taipan is the most venomous snake in the world – one bite contains enough venom to kill almost 250,000 mice – it avoids humans and is not aggressive like its close relative, the coastal taipan.

OPPOSITE:
Green tree python
This tree-dwelling species, *Morelia viridis*, lives in New Guinea, Australia and Indonesia. Green tree pythons spend their time coiled up on branches with their heads tucked in the middle.

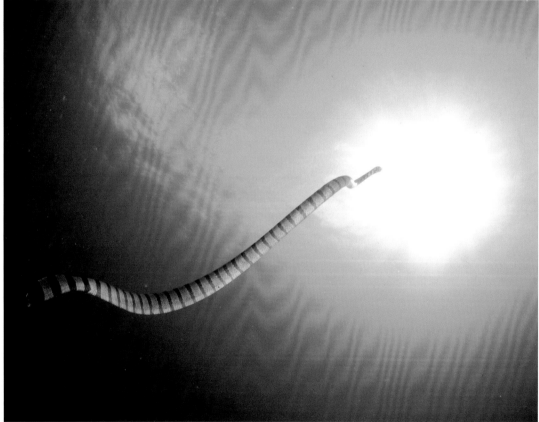

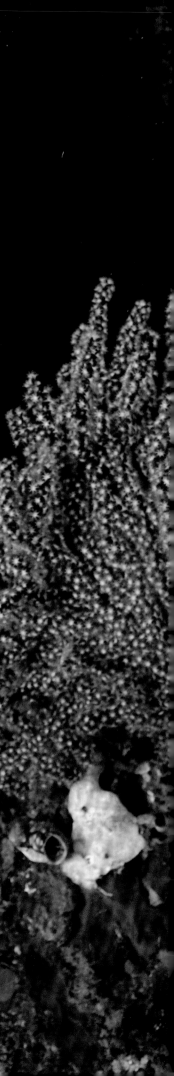

ALL PHOTOGRAPHS:
Belcher's sea snake
Among the most poisonous snakes, this sea snake species (*Hydrophis belcheri*) belongs to the Elapidae family, also known as elapids. Members of this family also include cobras and mambas. *H. belcheri* is named after the explorer Sir Edward Belcher, who first discovered the snake.

King brown snake
The Australian species *Pseudechis australis* is a venomous elapid snake. Despite its common name, the king brown snake belongs to the *Pseudechis* genus known as the black snakes. Their scales have two different colour tones, giving these snakes a reticulated pattern.

Eastern brown snake
This true brown snake of the
Pseudonaja genus is native to
eastern and central Australia and
southern New Guinea. The eastern
brown snake, or *Pseudonaja
textilis*, is the second most
venomous land snake in the world,
after the inland taipan.

Black-headed python
As the name suggests, this snake's
head is shiny black. The same
colour also extends down its neck.
The black-headed python, or
Aspidites melanocephalus, belongs
to the python family called
Pythonidae, and is non-venomous.

Black-naped snake
Neelaps bimaculatus gets its name
from the two distinctive black
patches on its head and the back
of its neck. This venomous snake
can be found in burrows in South
and Western Australia.

OPPOSITE BOTTOM:

In shed

A carpet python sheds its outer skin. When snakes are about to shed, their eyes look cloudy or blue, impairing their vision. This may result in aggressive behaviour.

LEFT TOP:

Carpet python

This tree-dwelling python, *Morelia spilota*, can reach a length of 2–4m (6.6–13ft) and weigh up to 15kg (33lb). It is found in Australia, New Guinea, the Bismarck Archipelago and the Solomon Islands.

LEFT BOTTOM:

Feeding

Like all members of the Pythonidae family, the carpet python is non-venomous and kills its prey by constriction. Here, a carpet python feeds on a rat, which it will swallow whole.

OVERLEAF:

Scrub python

Simalia amethistina, or the amethystine python, lives in Papua New Guinea and Indonesia. Also known as the scrub python, this snake is the largest in Papua New Guinea and can measure more than 9m (29.5ft) in length.

Physical agility
An Australian tree snake slithers up a tree. These slender, large-eyed snakes can be yellow or green, black and sometimes blue. Looking more closely, their yellow scales on the flanks have splashes of blue.

Australian tree snake
This rare blue-coloured snake, *Dendrelaphis punctulatus*, can be found in Australia and Papua New Guinea. It is non-venomous and goes by many common names: Australian tree snake, common tree snake and green tree snake.

Bandy-bandy snakes
This Australian snake, with black and white bands along its entire body, is a member of the *Vermicella* genus. There are six species of *Vermicella*, commonly known as the bandy-bandies or hoop snakes, often recognized by their location.

RIGHT TOP:

Coastal taipan

One of the most venomous snakes, the species *Oxyuranus scutellatus* is native to New Guinea and the coastal regions of northern and eastern Australia.

RIGHT MIDDLE:

Oviparous

Coastal taipans lay clutches of 7–20 eggs, generally in abandoned animal burrows. Females can store sperm from the males and produce a second clutch, often months after mating. Animals, like this female coastal taipan, that reproduce by laying eggs are called oviparous.

RIGHT BOTTOM:

Hatching time

This newly hatched coastal taipan is 30–34cm (12–13in) long. It took about two to three months for the egg to hatch, but now the hatchling will grow quickly, reaching 1m (3.3ft) in length in a year.

FAR RIGHT:

On their own

These young coastal taipans are ready to live on their own after hatching. It takes around 28 months for the females to reach sexual maturity, while males mature at around 16 months of age.

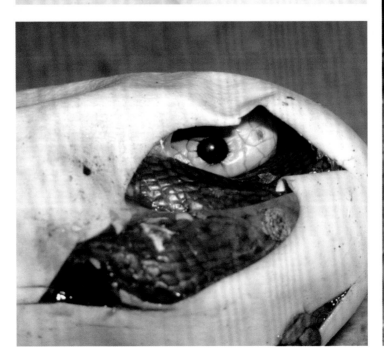

ABOVE TOP:
White-lipped snake
Native to southeastern Australia and Tasmania, the white-lipped snake (*Drysdalia coronoides*) gets its name from a thin white line on its upper lip. This line is bordered by another thin black line.

ABOVE BOTTOM:
Rough-scaled snake
As the name suggests, this venomous snake's scales have a ridge down the centre, making them rough or keeled. The rough-scaled snake, or *Tropidechis carinatus*, spreads from New South Wales to the tip of Queensland, Australia.

RIGHT:
Jungle carpet python
This beautiful black and yellow python is a subspecies of the carpet python. Known as *Morelia spilota cheynei*, or the jungle carpet python, it lives in the rainforests of Queensland in Australia.

ABOVE TOP:

Dubois' sea snake

Named after Belgian naturalist Charles Frédéric Dubois, *Aipysurus duboisii* is the world's most venomous sea snake. Found in tropical waters, it lives mostly in coral reefs at sea depths up to 80m (262ft) and preys on moray eels and fish.

ABOVE BOTTOM:

Inland taipan

Oxyuranus microlepidotus, commonly known as the inland taipan, is the most venomous snake in the world. Inland taipans are reclusive and rare, usually tucked away in clay cracks and crevices of Queensland and South Australia's floodplains.

RIGHT:

Southern desert banded snake

With a shovel-shaped snout, the Australian species *Simoselaps bertholdi* often buries itself in loose sand. Like all members of the *Simoselaps* genus – commonly known as the Australian coral snakes – the southern desert banded snake, or Jan's banded snake, is venomous.

Rough-scaled python
As the name suggests, this tree-dwelling python has corrugated scales. This helps the rough-scaled python (*Morelia carinata*) to climb trees and sandstone crevices. It is rare and can be found in parts of Western Australia.

OPPOSITE:

Triangular head

The rough-scaled python, or *Morelia carinata*, is usually dark brown with light brown blotches and has a triangular head and narrow neck. It reaches about 2m (6.6 ft) in length.

ABOVE TOP:

Northern death adder

Though this cryptic snake resembles a viper, it actually belongs to the Elapidae family. Found in Australia and Papua New Guinea, the northern death adder (*Acanthophis praelongus*) is very venomous and lures its prey by wiggling its tail like a worm.

ABOVE BOTTOM:

Red-bellied black snake

One of eastern Australia's most common snakes, the venomous red-bellied black snake (*Pseudechis porphyriacus*) is often found near shallow waters such as lagoons, hunting its main prey, frogs. In spring, males put on a fight show to win over females, and even have head-pushing contests.

ABOVE TOP:
Tongue flicking
Snakes use their tongues to
gather information about their
surroundings. By flicking them in
and out, they pick up chemical
molecules from the air and ground,
which can then be 'smelled' by a
pair of organs located on the roof
of their mouths.

ABOVE BOTTOM:
Shelter
The ringed brown snake lives in
arid shrublands and grasslands
of inland Australia, from western
New South Wales and Queensland
to Western Australia. Here, a
young ringed brown snake hides
amongst tree litter.

RIGHT:
Ringed brown snake
This venomous snake (*Pseudonaja
modesta*) resembles its close
relative, the eastern brown snake.
However, the ringed brown snake
has four to seven black rings
dispersed across its body. It grows
up to about 50cm (20in) long.

Smooth-scaled death adder
This cryptic species, *Acanthophis laevis*, gets its shiny and glossy look from its smooth scales. The so-called smooth-scaled death adder is venomous and can inconspicuously ambush its prey. It can be found in Papua New Guinea and Indonesia.

OPPOSITE AND ABOVE:
Common death adder
The Australian species *Acanthophis antarcticus*, or common death adder, sits and waits for prey such as frogs, lizards and birds to come to it. In fact, it blends in with its surroundings and uses its grub-like tail to lure in prey, before striking and injecting its deadly venom into them.

LEFT MIDDLE AND BOTTOM:
Desert death adder
This brick-red or yellow-reddish venomous snake, with yellow bands and a flattened triangular head, can blend perfectly into its environment. It is known as the desert death adder, or *Acanthophis pyrrhus*, and lives in Australia.

RIGHT:
Black-striped burrowing snake
At no more than 28cm (11in) long, this beautiful snake is Australia's smallest venomous snake. The black-striped burrowing snake, or *Neelaps calonotos*, is named for the black stripe on its back, which runs down its body and tail.

OPPOSITE:
Australian coral snake
Also known as the eastern shovel-nosed snake or *Brachyurophis australis*, this venomous coral snake from Australia uses its nose to dig itself into the sand. It is quite small, reaching up to 38cm (15in) in length.

ABOVE TOP:

Woma python

This Australian species, *Aspidites ramsayi*, catches most of its prey in burrows. However, due to lack of space, this requires the woma python to push a coil against the animal rather than wrapping its coils around it.

ABOVE BOTTOM AND RIGHT:

Tiger snakes

Members of the *Notechis* genus are known as tiger snakes for their black and yellow stripes. However, tiger snakes do not always live up to their name. Some have different-coloured patterns, while others are entirely patternless. When threatened, these venomous snakes from Australia can flatten their bodies considerably.

North America

The North American continent comprises Canada, the United States, Mexico, Central America and the Caribbean. Geographically, Greenland is also part of this continent – though no snakes roam around this island. Deserts, forests, mountains, swamps and everything in between occupy this continent, along with incredibly diverse animals. Snakes are found throughout most of North America, from the southern half of Canada down to Central America and the Caribbean.

The venomous rattlesnakes, such as the sidewinders and diamondback rattlesnakes, are only found in the Americas. These snakes are well known for making a rattling noise with the end of their tails as a warning. Some non-venomous snakes, such as the black rat snakes and gopher snakes, mimic rattlesnakes by moving their tails against the ground. The harmless and often colourful garter snakes are another species of snake living only in North America, while the eastern indigo snakes are the continent's largest native species.

The iridescent scales of rainbow boas, which refract light like small prisms and create a rainbow, will undoubtedly hypnotize you in Central and South America. And though they look like worms, the slender blind snakes or threadsnakes, are some of North America's smallest snakes.

OPPOSITE:
Checkered garter snake
The black checkerboard pattern down this greenish snake's back gives it its name. The checkered garter snake (*Thamnophis marcianus*) can be found in deserts or grasslands of southwestern United States, Mexico and Central America.

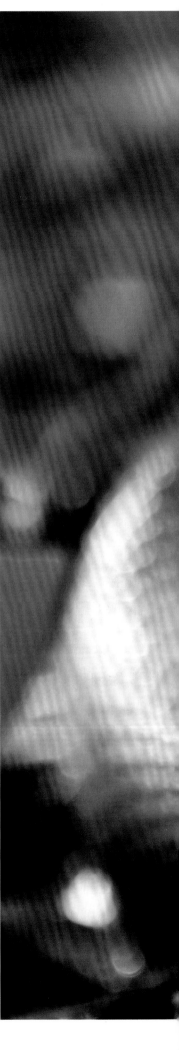

ABOVE TOP:
Milk snakes
Named after the false belief that
they milked cows, milk snakes
spread from southeastern Canada
to South America. There are 24
subspecies of the harmless species
Lampropeltis triangulum, many
of which strikingly resemble the
extremely venomous coral snakes,
to scare away predators.

ABOVE BOTTOM:
Pacific gopher snake
The subspecies *Pituophis catenifer
catenifer*, which has the distinctive
feature of two to three rows of
spots on its sides, is native to the
western coast of North America.
When they are threatened, the
harmless gopher snakes mimic
rattlesnakes and 'rattle' their tails
against the ground.

RIGHT:
Black rat snake
The non-venomous species
Pantherophis obsoletus, found
in central North America, is an
excellent climber. Besides this
usual black colour, there is a
brown-to-black variant called the
Texas rat snake.

Blotched palm-pit viper
This beguiling species, *Bothriechis supraciliaris*, inhabits the mountainous area of southwestern Costa Rica. Like all members of the *Bothriechis* genus – commonly known as palm-pit vipers – it is venomous. The blotched part of its name is apt; it has irregular blotches on its back that sometimes form crossbands.

OPPOSITE TOP AND BOTTOM:
Blunthead tree snake
This long, slender, tree-dwelling
snake, with a large head and big
eyes, is known as the blunthead
tree snake or *Imantodes cenchoa*.
It can grow to about 1.5m (5ft)
long and its large eyes make up
about a quarter of its head!

ABOVE:
Antiguan racer
Among the world's rarest, this
critically endangered species,
Alsophis antiguae, used to be
found only on a tiny private
island off the coast of Antigua
called Great Bird Island. With
conservation efforts, however,
it now also lives on the nearby
Rabbit Island, Green Island and
York Island.

Puffing snake
This non-venomous species, *Phrynonax poecilonotus*, is one of the most variable snakes in the world. Throughout its life, it continuously changes colours – from a dull colour when it hatches to a slate grey or black with yellow, orange, red or light pinkish-purple. *P. poecilonotus* lives across Mexico, Central America and South America.

167

Central American coral snake
The colourful bands of this extremely venomous snake can vary from black and red to black, red and yellow. Its snout is always black. Central American coral snakes, or *Micrurus nigrocinctus*, can be found in Mexico, Central America and South America.

Red-tailed coral snake
As the common name suggests, the extremely venomous species *Micrurus mipartitus* has three to four red tail rings. The second ring on its head is also red, as opposed to the white bands on the rest of its body.

Hearing
A Costa Rican coral snake slithers down a flower. Though snakes do not have external ears or eardrums like we do, their inner ears are well developed. So, while slithering away, they pick up vibrations from the ground and air through their lower jawbones and can 'hear'.

Costa Rican coral snake
Found in Nicaragua, Costa Rica and Panama, the Costa Rican coral snake (*Micrurus mosquitensis*) is deadly. It can be recognized by its distinctive yellow rings on either side of the black rings.

LEFT:
Breeding ball
Many garter males, like these red-sided garter snakes or *Thamnophis sirtalis parietalis*, often try to mate with one female, resulting in a breeding ball.

ABOVE TOP:
Garter snakes
All members of the *Thamnophis* genus are known as garter snakes. These snakes, native to North and Central America, comprise about 35 species and subspecies. Not only do they look quite different but their size also varies, measuring between 45cm and 130cm (1.5ft and 4.3ft).

ABOVE BOTTOM:
Ovoviviparous
A female eastern garter snake, *Thamnophis sirtalis sirtalis*, gives birth to live young. Some snake species are ovoviviparous, which means that females first incubate the eggs inside their bodies and then give birth to live young.

OPPOSITE:

Black-speckled palm-pit viper
This distinctive emerald green
snake with black blotches is the
black-speckled palm-pit viper or
Bothriechis nigroviridis. It can be
found in the mountains of Costa
Rica and Panama.

ABOVE:

Northern Pacific rattlesnake
Crotalus oreganus, from western
North America, comes out of its
burrow. This venomous pit viper
uses the heat-sensing pits on its
face to locate prey such as birds,
mice and rabbits.

ABOVE TOP:

Blackneck garter snake
Thamnophis cyrtopsis, or the blackneck garter snake, is native to southwestern United States, Mexico and Guatemala. It is often found near water, preying on fish, frogs, earthworms and other snakes.

ABOVE BOTTOM:

Plains garter snake
One of the most cold-tolerant snakes, the plains garter snake (*Thamnophis radix*) often basks in the sun even on warmer winter days. It is found near water across the United States.

RIGHT:

Eastern copperhead
The venomous pit viper, *Agkistrodon contortrix*, is commonly found across the United States and northern Mexico. Unsurprisingly, the copperhead gets its name from its bronze-hued head.

OPPOSITE:

Yellow-blotched palm-pit viper
This beautiful green snake with black-bordered yellow blotches is the yellow-blotched palm-pit viper, or *Bothriechis aurifer*. It can be found in Mexico and Guatemala, often in trees, grasping branches with its prehensile tail.

LEFT:

Northern watersnake
Northern watersnakes, or *Nerodia sipedon*, can often be seen basking on stumps, rocks and shrubs, or hunting at the water's edges during the day and at night.

BELOW:

Florida green watersnake
At about 0.76–1.4m (2.5–4.6ft), *Nerodia floridana* is the longest watersnake in North America. Here, a mass of Florida green watersnakes are mating in spring.

Egg tooth
Corn snakes hatch from their eggs. About 10 weeks after a female corn snake lays a clutch of 12–24 eggs, the hatchlings use an egg tooth to break out of the shell, which is later shed. The hatchling corn snakes that emerge are about 13cm (5in) long.

ALL PHOTOGRAPHS:
Corn snakes
This stunning species of rat snake, *Pantherophis guttatus*, is found across southeastern and central United States. Often mistaken for the venomous copperhead, corn snakes are thinner, have round pupils and brighter colours, and lack heat-sensing pits. They make popular pets and through selective breeding come in a wide variety of colours and patterns.

OPPOSITE:
Prehensile tail
A beautiful tree-dwelling eyelash viper, or *Bothriechis schlegelii*, dangles from a branch. To do this, it uses its prehensile tail, which is adapted to grasp or hold.

LEFT AND BELOW:
Sidewinder
The rattlesnake species *Crotalus cerastes* lives in the deserts of southwestern United States and northwestern Mexico. Also known as the horned rattlesnake, its horn-like scales above its eyes prevent sand from falling into them when buried beneath it. *C. cerastes* moves quickly on sand by coiling part of its body into a loop and hurling it forwards – a method called sidewinding.

ABOVE TOP:
Eastern indigo snake
The blue-black *Drymarchon couperi* is the longest native snake in North America. Sometimes it has a reddish-orange face, like this one here. The longest eastern indigo snake measured 2.8m (9.2ft) in length.

ABOVE BOTTOM:
Brumation
In the winter, black-tailed rattlesnakes are commonly found huddling together sleeping in dens, often with other rattlesnake species, too. This activity is known as brumation and allows ectothermic or cold-blooded animals to conserve vital energy.

RIGHT:
Western diamondback rattlesnake
Members of the *Crotalus* genus are venomous vipers known as rattlesnakes. Like all rattlesnakes, the western diamondback rattlesnake, or *Crotalus atrox*, has a rattle at the tip of its tail, which it uses to warn off predators. Responsible for the majority of venomous snakebites in North America, they live in southwestern United States and Mexico.

BELOW TOP:

Mexican west coast boa constrictor

Only found in western Mexico, the species *Boa sigma* is protected by locals of Sonora because they believe that it is the guardian of water. It is similar to its close relatives, the boa constrictor and common boa.

BELOW BOTTOM:

Mexican vine snake

This very slender snake with a prominent snout, seen from Arizona through to northern South America, can often be mistaken as a vine. Here, a Mexican vine snake, or *Oxybelis aeneus*, opens its mouth – which is black inside – to intimidate a predator.

RIGHT:

Gray-banded kingsnake

This non-venomous snake, with orange-red and grey bands, is the gray-banded kingsnake or *Lampropeltis alterna*. It can be found across southwestern United States and Mexico.

LEFT:
Brown rainbow boa
Known for its iridescent scales, the brown rainbow boa (*Epicrates maurus*) lives mainly in rainforests in southern Central America, Trinidad and Tobago, and northern South America. At night, it hunts by ambushing prey, such as mice, birds and lizards, and swallows them whole.

ABOVE TOP:
Mexican west coast rattlesnake
At about 1.5m (4.9ft) or more, the western Mexican species *Crotalus basiliscus* is one of the largest rattlesnakes. Its specific name *basiliscus* is derived from the Greek for 'little king'.

ABOVE BOTTOM:
Bluestripe ribbon snake
The subspecies *Thamnophis sauritus nitae* can only be found along the northwest coast of Florida. Living near water, it is commonly known as the bluestripe ribbon snake for its two blue stripes and long, slender body that resembles a ribbon.

RIGHT TOP:

Ring-necked snake

As the common name suggests, the
harmless ring-necked snake has
a distinct yellow, red or yellow-
orange ring on its neck. This
species, *Diadophis punctatus*,
curls up its tail and shows off its
yellow-orange to red belly when it
is threatened.

RIGHT BOTTOM:

Rubber boa

This North American species,
Charina bottae, has a rubber-like
look. Commonly known as the
rubber boa, the snake is usually
tan to dark brown but can also be
olive-green, yellow or orange.

OPPOSITE:

Southern hog-nosed snake

Found in southeastern United
States, the southern hog-nosed
snake, or *Heterodon simus*, has a
small, stout body and a distinctive
upturned snout. When threatened,
it flattens its neck and raises its
head off the ground, similar to a
cobra, and hisses.

ABOVE TOP:
Desert rosy boa
The species *Lichanura trivirgata*, from southwestern United States
and northwestern Mexico, is one of the slowest-moving in the world.
However, the desert rosy boa strikes quickly and precisely when prey
is close.

ABOVE BOTTOM:
Coastal rosy boa
Lichanura orcutti, or the coastal rosy boa, lives in rocky habitats across
the southwestern parts of the United States. Coastal rosy boas get their
name from their rosy-coloured bellies – though in fact most individuals
lack this colouration.

RIGHT:
Texas rat snake
The subspecies *Pantherophis obsoletus lindheimeri* lives mainly in
Texas, but can also be found in Louisiana, Arkansas and Oklahoma.
It is a brown-to-black variant of the black rat snake, often with tinges
of orange or red. However, this Texas rat snake is white, or leucistic,
because of a genetic mutation.

South America

The continent of South America is teeming with distinctive plants and animals. Its vast tropical rainforests make this continent one of the most biodiverse. Snakes here come in dazzling colours and patterns, like the rare checker-bellied snake, the beautiful eyelash viper, or the emerald tree boa that changes from bright red-orange to green as it ages. Whereas North America is home to the tiniest snake, the Barbados threadsnake, South America has the largest in the world – by weight.

South America's green anacondas are extraordinarily long and bulky, though their length has often been exaggerated in the past. Their relatives, yellow or Paraguayan anacondas, are also quite large. So are the non-venomous boa constrictors, which can tightly wrap around wild pigs and deer, and the venomous bushmasters. Bushmasters, along with lanceheads and rattlesnakes, are some of the most venomous snakes in this part of the world. These are part of a larger group of ambush predator snakes known as Crotalinae, or pit vipers and crotaline snakes, distinguished for their heat-sensing vision. Many young crotalines have brightly coloured tails that contrast with the rest of their bodies, which are often used to lure unsuspecting prey.

OPPOSITE:
Cryptic
This long and slender tiger rat snake, or *Spilotes pullatus*, typically lives in tall trees. Its distinctive colour pattern helps it blend in with the sunlight speckles on the trees.

Tiger rat snake
One of the largest snakes in the Americas, *Spilotes pullatus* grows to 2.7m (8.9ft) long. It spreads from southern Mexico through Central America and across most of South America to northern Argentina. It also lives in Trinidad and Tobago.

ABOVE:
Yellow-bellied puffing snake
Spilotes sulphureus is one of largest snakes in the Americas, reaching up to 3m (9.8ft) in length. The yellow-bellied puffing snake has a yellow belly, as its name suggests, and a yellow-greenish back. This helps the snake stay hidden from predators and prey in the forests of Trinidad and Tobago and northern South America.

RIGHT:
Venom
The yellow-bellied puffing snake, also known as the Amazon puffing snake, has developed two types of venom that target different prey: one for killing small mammals, such as rats, and another for birds and lizards. Another mechanism, to keep any predators away, is that it blows up its bright yellow throat when alarmed.

False coral snake
Also known as the calico or forest flame snake, the mildly venomous species *Oxyrhopus petolarius* lives in the forests and savannahs of Central and South America. Its teeth are located in the back of its mouth, meaning its venom is toxic to small prey but harmless to us.

ABOVE AND OPPOSITE:
Heat-sensitive organs
Members of the Crotalinae subfamily are venomous snakes known as pit vipers. Pit vipers, like this two-striped forest pitviper from South America, have a pair of heat-sensitive organs located in openings, or pits, between the eyes and nostrils. These help them to detect warm-blooded prey such as mice in total darkness.

RIGHT:
Variegated snail-eater
This harmless South American species, *Dipsas variegata*, spends most of its time in trees. It feeds on snails and slugs, as its common name suggests, by following them or tracking their scent trails.

ABOVE TOP:

Amazon tree boa

The tree-dwelling species *Corallus hortulana*, from the Amazon, goes by many names: Amazon tree boa, macabrel and garden tree boa. It also comes in many colours and patterns, from black, grey or brown to green, yellow, orange and red, and any combination of these. Here, an Amazon tree boa sheds its old skin.

ABOVE BOTTOM:

Sharp teeth

Amazon tree boas have long front teeth. This helps them grasp birds, whilst biting through the feathers. Like pit vipers and pythons, boas also have heat-sensing pit organs so that they can hunt at night.

RIGHT:

Ready to strike

An Amazon tree boa uses its prehensile tail to hold on to the branch and take an S-shaped pose, ready to strike at its prey, such as birds, rats and bats. Though non-venomous, this species is aggressive and can attack without warning.

ABOVE TOP AND BOTTOM:

Green anaconda

Weighing up to 227kg (500lb), this massive boa species, *Eunectes murinus*, is the heaviest snake in the world. It is also one of the longest, but the reticulated python in Asia can reach greater lengths. Green anacondas spend most of their time in water and use their long, muscular bodies to constrict various prey, such as turtles, fish, deer and capybaras.

RIGHT:

Green vine snake

The long, slender species *Oxybelis fulgidus* lives in northern parts of South America and Central America. This tree-dwelling snake is not to be confused with members of the Ahaetulla genus found in Asia, which are also known as green vine snakes.

ABOVE:
Checker-bellied snake
This beautiful and rare species, *Siphlophis cervinus*, lives across the Amazon rainforest of South America, as well as in Trinidad and Tobago.

RIGHT, FAR RIGHT AND OPPOSITE:
New world species
These coral snakes from South America are members of the *Micrurus* genus. This is one of the genera in the Elapidae family, commonly known as elapids, which totals about 360 species of venomous snakes.

RIGHT TOP:

Common neckband snake

The species *Scaphiodontophis venustissimus* can be found across both Central and South America. It is one of the most accomplished mimickers of the venomous coral snake, with yellow rings around the black rings.

RIGHT MIDDLE:

Parrot snake

This slender snake (*Leptophis ahaetulla*), with a bright green and bronze body, lives in South and Central America. There are 10 known parrot snake subspecies, all of which are mildly venomous but not enough to affect humans.

RIGHT BOTTOM:

Southern American bushmaster

The viper species *Lachesis muta* resembles a rattlesnake. Its tail has a spiny end, which it vigorously vibrates when threatened. However, it has no rattle and gets its name *muta* from the Latin for 'mute'. At almost 3.65m (12ft) long, it is the third longest venomous snake after the king cobra in Asia and black mamba in Africa.

OPPOSITE:

Common lancehead

This easily agitated species, *Bothrops atrox*, lives in the tropical lowlands of South America. Often confused with its close relative, *Terciopelo* or *Bothrops asper*, the common lancehead usually has rectangular blotches. It can give live birth to up to 80 snakes at once!

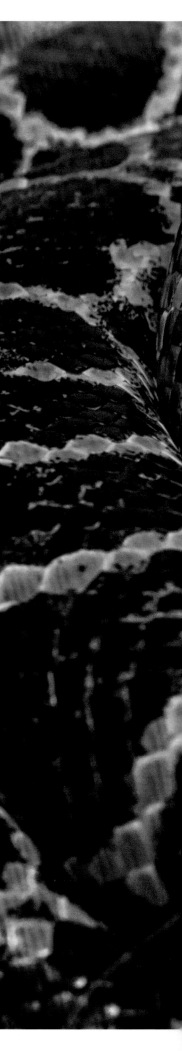

ABOVE BOTTOM:

Yellow-tailed cribo
Named for its black back with a
blue glow and a yellow tail, the
indigo snake or yellow-tailed cribo
(*Drymarchon corais*) reaches
over 2m (6.6ft) in length. It can
typically be found in forested areas
of South America.

ABOVE TOP AND RIGHT:

Paraguayan anaconda
A close-up of the head of the
Paraguayan anaconda, *Eunectes
notaeus*, shows the nostrils and
eyes on the top of its head. This is
so the snake can breathe and see
while swimming. Also known as
the yellow anaconda, *E. notaeus*
lives near water like its bigger close
relative, the green anaconda.

South American rattlesnake
This beautiful pit viper subspecies, *Crotalus durissus durissus*, lives on the coastal savannahs of Guyana, French Guiana and Suriname. It is an extremely venomous snake, and is most active at dawn and dusk, when it hunts for mainly rodents.

OPPOSITE:

Emerald tree boa

This non-venomous, reddish-orange juvenile snake will gradually turn emerald green, as its name suggests. An adult emerald tree boa, or *Corallus caninus*, closely resembles the green tree python (*Morelia viridis*) from Southeast Asia and Australia.

LEFT TOP:

Dark-spotted anaconda

Native to northeastern South America, the non-venomous constrictor *Eunectes deschauenseei* can usually be found near water. *E. deschauenseei* is named after American ornithologist Rodolphe Meyer de Schauensee.

LEFT MIDDLE:

Eyelash viper

This yellow venomous viper is named for the eyelash-like scales above its eyes. Measuring 55–82cm (22–32in) long, the eyelash viper, or *Bothriechis schlegelii*, is relatively small. It lives in Central and South America.

LEFT BOTTOM:

Brazilian smooth snake

The giant species *Hydrodynastes gigas* can reach more than 3m (9.9ft) in length. Also known as the false water cobra, it flattens its neck into a hood like a cobra.

ABOVE TOP:

Common boa

Often confused with the boa constrictor, *Boa imperator* usually has a darker brown or red tail. Even so, it is mistakenly called the red-tailed boa. It belongs to the Boidae family, known as boas or boids, which comprises non-venomous constrictors.

ABOVE BOTTOM:

Argentine boa

This subspecies, *Boa constrictor occidentalis*, is native to Argentina and Paraguay. It can only be found in the warm subtropical regions of these countries. Argentine boas vary in colour but are usually dark or black, and are large, like their close relative, the boa constrictor.

RIGHT:

Boa constrictor

The large, docile species *Boa constrictor* lives in tropical South America and some islands in the Caribbean. In the wild, the boa constrictor, also known as the red-tailed boa, rarely reaches 3m (9.9ft) in length, but can grow to 5m (16ft) in captivity.

Aruba rattlesnake
As the name suggests, this rare rattlesnake is found only on the Caribbean island of Aruba. The Aruba rattlesnake, or *Crotalus unicolor*, blends in wonderfully with its thorny scrubland and desert habitats. It grows to about 90cm (2.95ft) long and weighs about 1kg (2.2lb).